TABLE OF CONTENTS

Welcome to the PREHISTORIC HUNTERS!

Carnotaurus
(KAR-noh-TORE-uhss)

Ty
Tyrannosaurus rex
(tie-RAN-oh-SOR-uhss
RECKS)

Welcome back! It's me, Ty! Are you ready for a **3-D Dinosaur Discovery** adventure? We'll be heading back to the Mesozoic to check out some of the most dangerous dinos that ever lived—the **prehistoric hunters**. We'll meet meat-eaters big and small, get to know a few famous ones, and learn lots along the way! Did you know that:

◆ Some meat-eating dinos had teeth that were as big as bananas?

◆ There were dinos that could run as fast as a racehorse?

◆ Some dinos went fishing?

4

PREHISTORIC HUNTERS

Giganotosaurus
(JIG-uh-NOTE-oh-SOR-uhss)

by
Suzanne Francis

with
Matthew T. Carrano, Ph.D.
Consultant

Scholastic Inc.

New York   Toronto   London   Auckland   Sydney
Mexico City   New Delhi   Hong Kong   Buenos Aires

ISBN 0-439-83863-0

Designer: Lee Kaplan

Front cover and title page: *Giganotosaurus* © Jorge Blanco;
(blue forest) © Mellow Rapp/Shutterstock.com.

Back cover illustration: *Cryolophosaurus* © Jaime Chirinos.

All Ty the *Tyrannosaurus rex* illustrations by Ed Shems.

All 3-D conversions by Pinsharp 3D Graphics.

Photo and Illustration Credits:

Pages 4–5: *Carnotaurus* © Jaime Chirinos. (Editor's note: Since grass wasn't around during the Mesozoic, the artist has drawn the dinosaurs shown here in a field of dried-out ferns and other low-lying plants that grew in Patagonia, Argentina.)

Pages 6–7: *Carcharodontosaurus* © Julius Csotonyi; (tyrannosaur claw) © Kris Kripchak.

Page 8: *Carnotaurus* head © Jorge Blanco; (small theropod tooth) © Kris Kripchak.

Page 9: *Tyrannosaurus rex* © Joe Tucciarone; (*Allosaurus* skull) © B. Speckart/Shutterstock.com; (dinosaur skeleton) © Tonis Valing/Shutterstock.com.

Page 10: Two tyrannosaurs © Todd Marshall.

Page 11: Stripy *Tyrannosaurus rex* © Julius Csotonyi; (*T. rex* statue in Alberta, Canada) © Sue Sabrowski.

Page 12: *Rugops* © Todd Marshall.

Page 13: *Torvosaurus* and *Othnielia* © Todd Marshall.

Page 14–15: All photos © The Field Museum.

Page 16: *Allosaurus* and carcass © Gerhard Boeggemann.

Page 17: All photos © University of Wyoming Geological Museum.

Page 18: *Carnotaurus* tail © Jaime Chirinos.

Page 19: *Ceratosaurus* and prey © Jaime Chirinos.

Page 20: *Spinosaurus* © Joe Tucciarone.

Page 21: *Suchomimus* © Todd Marshall.

Page 22: (Dromaeosaur arms) © Kris Kripchak; (dinosaur icons) © Jafaris Mustafa/Shutterstock.com.

Page 23: *Coelophysis* © Todd Marshall; (raptor foot) © B. Speckart/Shutterstock.com.

Page 24–25: All dinosaur illustrations © Todd Marshall.

Page 26: (*Tenontosaurus* and *Deinonychus*) © Alan Groves.

Page 27: *Oviraptor* © Julius Csotonyi; (*Oviraptor* and babies) © Alan Groves.

Page 28–29: (*The Lost World*) © Photofest; (*The Lost World: Jurassic Park*) © Universal Studios/Amblin Entertainment/Photofest; (popcorn) © Samantha Grandy/Shutterstock.com; (filmstrip) © Mikhail/Shutterstock.com.

Page 30: (Yancy and Phillip in home workshop) photo courtesy of Yancy Calzada; (*Dinosaur*) © Walt Disney Pictures/Photofest.

Page 31: *Utahraptor* © Todd Marshall.

Page 32: Young *Carcharodontosaurus* and two small theropods © Gerhard Boeggemann.

12 11 10 9 8 7 6 5 4 3 2 1   6 7 8 9 10 11/0

Printed in the U.S.A.

First Scholastic printing, February 2006

And we'll answer some of the questions about these dinos like:

◆ **What kinds of hunting dinos lived in the Mesozoic?**

◆ **How did meat-eaters get their meals?**

◆ **Are dinos in movies and TV the real thing?**

 And don't forget—when you see this icon, put on your **3-D glasses** to see the dino picture pop!

Are you ready for a dino-riffic adventure? Follow the tracks and let's get started!

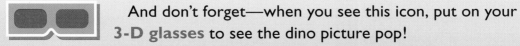

All meat-eating dinosaurs are **theropods** (THAYR-oh-pods), a group of dinos with some common traits. Check out these pages to find out more about this fierce group of dinos!

▲

Theropods weren't looking for plants and leaves to munch on. They were hunters—and dino hunters didn't eat anything green! That's because theropods are **carnivores** (KAR-nih-VORES).

That's right! No veggies for us theropods!

Dino Dictionary

A *carnivore* is an animal that only eats meat. You wouldn't catch a carnivore at a salad bar! An *herbivore* (ER-bih-VORE) is an animal that only eats plants.

▶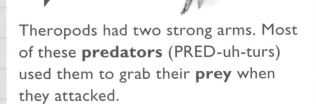

Theropods had two strong arms. Most of these **predators** (PRED-uh-turs) used them to grab their **prey** when they attacked.

Dino Dictionary

A *predator* hunts and kills other animals for food. The animals a predator kills and eats are its *prey*.

Theropods also had sharp, hooked claws at the ends of their fingers and toes. These claws were powered by super-strength to tear into prey and helped dinos protect themselves. Handy!

Tyrannosaur claw

WHAT IS A THEROPOD?

Carcharodontosaurus
(KAR-kar-roh-DON-toe-SOR-uhss)

Theropods had long, strong tails that weren't just for show! A tail made it possible for a dino to run, jump, and make sharp turns. Without one, a theropod would've done a nosedive right into the dirt! Ouch!

Theropods are **bipedal** (by-PED-uhl), which means they walked and ran on two feet. These dinos' legs had to be strong—some theropods weighed up to 6 tons!

DINO DATA

Some fossil hunters in Argentina clawed their way to a fantastic find: a 15-inch (38 cm) claw that belonged to a *Megaraptor* (MEG-uh-RAP-tore). Even though *Megaraptor* has a claw that looks like a raptor's (see page 23), this huge claw was on its hand, not its foot.

A Head Above the Rest

Carnotaurus

Compared to other dinos, theropods had very large heads—they needed a big noggin to hold some important hunting tools! Check out the picture for more info.

Some theropods had eyes that faced forward to give them better **depth perception**. These peepers might have made it easier for theropods to scope out their next meal!

Dino Dictionary

Depth perception is what lets you see in 3-D. It helps you tell if something is close or far away.

Some scientists think that theropods had a super sense of smell. Their high-powered sniffer could've helped them find meals over long distances.

Theropods had incredibly strong jaws for biting and killing prey. These jaws had a special feature: an extra-flexible jaw joint. This joint let their jaws open extra wide for a super-sized bite.

Most theropods had a mouthful of sharp teeth for plenty of meat eatin'! Each tooth was like a steak knife with a sharp, jagged edge. And no dentists for these dinos—if a tooth broke or fell out, another one grew back in.

We're good friends with the tooth fairy!

Small theropod tooth

HOOD ORNAMENTS

You might've noticed that some theropods had some strange decorations on their heads, like the *Carnotaurus* on this page. Scientists think that these horns and ridges weren't for fighting or catching prey. Instead, they helped theropods tell one another apart or scared off rivals.

HUGE 'N' HUNGRY: BIG THEROPODS

Tyrannosaurus rex

Tyrannosaurus rex

In 1902, a dino hunter named Barnum Brown made a spectacular find while digging in Hell Creek, Montana. He dug up a meat-eating dino that was the biggest anyone had ever seen! This dino was named **Tyrannosaurus rex**, which means "tyrant lizard king."

No bones about it—*Tyrannosaurus rex* (or *T. rex*, for short) was an awesome theropod. People all over the world love this dino—it's a superstar! Read on to find out more about one of the most famous dinos of all time.

THE BARE BONES

Name: *Tyrannosaurus rex*

Time period: Late Cretaceous—65 million years ago

Size: A full-grown *T. rex* was up to 42 feet (13 m) long, 15 feet (4½ m) tall, and could weigh up to 7 tons. That's as big as a bus and as heavy as an adult elephant!

Regions found: Most *T. rex* fossils have been found in western states of the U.S., like Montana, Wyoming, and the Dakotas.

Two tyrannosaurs

How much do you know about the almighty *T. rex*? Test yourself! Try to guess if the facts on these pages are **true** or **false**. Then turn the page upside down to get the real scoop on this prehistoric hunter!

1. *T. rex* was the largest meat-eating dinosaur that ever lived.

False. *T. rex* was named "king of the dinosaurs" because it was the biggest carnivore known back then. But in 1993, another fossil was discovered in Argentina. *Giganotosaurus* was almost the same size as *T. rex*. It was a little bit longer, but not as heavy.

2. *T. rex* could outrun a car!

False. People used to think that *T. rex* was a speedy runner. They thought it could sprint up to 40 miles (64 km) per hour! But *T. rex* probably wasn't so speedy. Based on new info, we think it could probably only run 10–15 miles (16–24 km) per hour.

Pop Quiz: *T. Rex True or False*

3. *T. rex* had a mouthful of 60 teeth—each tooth was as big as a banana.

True. *T. rexes* did have up to 60 teeth. Each tooth was up to 7 inches (18 cm) long—and about the size and shape of a banana.

4. A *T. rex* could swallow an adult human whole.

True. A *T. rex* could fit 200 pounds (91 kg) of food in one bite. That's one mega-mouthful!

5. A *T. rex*'s arm and a person's arm are the same size.

True. Hard to believe, but it's true. Compared to the rest of its body, *T. rex* arms were tiny!

6. Each of a *T. rex*'s arms could lift up to 450 pounds (204 kg).

True. Scientists don't know what *T. rexes* used their arms for, but whatever it was, they needed major muscle for it!

7. *T. rex* was striped like a zebra.

Don't Know! Fossilized dino skin is rare, and even when scientists do find it, they can't tell what color it was. Could be true, could be false.

A stripy *Tyrannosaurus rex*

We could've had polka dots!

DON'T DRAG YOUR TAIL!

You might see some old pictures of a *T. rex* standing upright and dragging its tail. Nowadays scientists think *T. rex* held its tail *off* the ground to help balance its heavy body over its two legs (like the pic on page 10). Any other way, and this dino would've just fallen over!

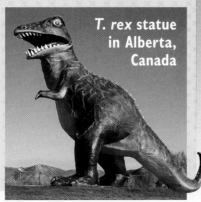

T. rex statue in Alberta, Canada

Q: What do you get when a dino walks through a parking lot?

A: *Tyrannosaurus* wrecks!

A Dino Debate

You'd think a dino like a *T. rex* could snap up a snack in a flash, but you'd be surprised! Scientists are still trying to figure out if *T. rex* was a **hunter** or a **scavenger** (SCAV-en-jer). Check out the facts on both sides of this dino debate.

Scientists think that *Rugops* (ROOG-ahps), shown on the left, might have been a scavenging dino

Strolling Scavengers

◆ A *T. rex*'s legs were made for **walking long distances, not chasing prey**. Scientists guess that the top speed for a *T. rex* was about 10–15 miles (16–24 km) per hour. *T. rexes* were strolling, not sprinting!

◆ *T. rex*'s short arms weren't very handy! With only **two fingers per hand**, *T. rexes* probably couldn't get much of a grip on anything!

◆ Scientists do have fossils with *T. rex* teeth marks in them, but what would really prove that *T. rexes* were hunters is **if there were dino fossils with *T. rex* bites that healed**. This would mean that *T. rex* hunted a live lunch, but it got away. Scientists haven't found this piece of the puzzle just yet!

Hungry Hunters

◆ *T. rex* may not have been the fastest dino, but **it was probably much speedier than some of the slow-moving herbivores** back in the Cretaceous. *T. rex* definitely could've made the catch of the day!

◆ *T. rex* had a **big head with strong jaws**—these would have been very useful for attacking *live* prey.

◆ **T. rex wasn't the only hunter without useful hands out there.** Sharks, birds, and snakes dine on fresh meat without the help of hands at all!

DINO DOUBLE DUTY

Most large predators alive today, like lions, will scavenge meat, even though they prefer fresh. Maybe *T. rex* hunted when there weren't any leftovers around!

A *Torvosaurus* (TORE-voh-SOR-uhss) hunts an *Othnielia* (OHTH-neel-lee-uh)

13

A *T. rex* Named Sue

In 1990, a fossil hunter named Susan Hendrickson was exploring a cliff in South Dakota when she discovered some very interesting bones. A *lot* of interesting bones—it took three weeks for her and a team of paleontologists to dig them up! Those bones turned out to be the find of a lifetime—an almost complete *Tyrannosaurus rex*! The team named the fossil "Sue," after its discoverer. There are only a handful of *T. rex* skeletons out there, but none of them are as complete as Sue.

Sue's really got it together!

A model of what Sue might have looked like

SUE'S STATS

Found: August 12, 1990 in South Dakota

Age: Late Cretaceous—67 million years old

Sex: Unknown. Some scientists think that Sue is a female because of her size, but we really don't know.

Sue's Skull

Dinosaur skulls are very rare because they fall apart much faster than other bones. Sue's skull was in great condition—including the more delicate bones. This makes Sue an ex-skull-ent specimen!

A T-weet Rex

Some scientists think that Sue's skeleton has a wishbone, just like a bird and some other theropods. This would be the first wishbone found on a *T. rex* and it would support the idea that birds are related to dinosaurs.

Sue's skull

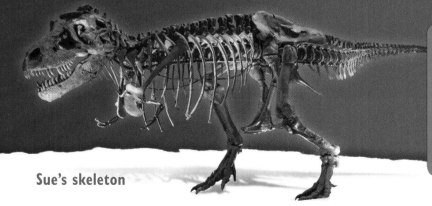

Sue's skeleton

DINO DATA

The Field Museum in Chicago, Illinois (where Sue calls home), shelled out $8.4 million for Sue's bones—that's the most ever paid for a fossil!

Size: 42 feet (13 m) long and 13 feet (4 m) tall. To date, Sue is the largest *T. rex* fossil ever found. She's about as long as the Statue of Liberty's right arm!

Weight When Alive: 7 tons

Number of Bones: Over 300 fossilized bones make Sue 90 percent complete!

Number of Teeth: 58. One of Sue's teeth is 7 inches (18 cm) long. That's the longest *T. rex* tooth ever found!

Health: Scientists found evidence of arthritis on Sue's old bones and noticed poorly healed broken ribs. Turn to page 18 to read more on how life wasn't easy for big meat-eaters!

Allosaurus and carcass

Allosaurus

Tyrannosaurus rex might have been the king of the Cretaceous, but ***Allosaurus*** (AL-oh-SOR-uhss) was the king of the Jurassic. These two dinos never met because they were separated by 50 million years!

It's too bad Al and I have never met. We have a lot in common!

Big Al

In 1991, paleontologists in Wyoming made an exciting discovery: a well-preserved *Allosaurus* skeleton. Scientists named the 145 million-year-old fossil "Big Al." Big Al wasn't full-grown, but he is the most complete *Allosaurus* fossil ever found—about 95 percent complete! Most dinos are only known by one or two bones, so Al's truly a fantastic find!

Big Al at the University of Wyoming Geological Museum in Laramie, Wyoming

Scientists think the big bump on Big Al's middle toe was from a bad infection

Hard Prehistoric Times

Along with its size and shape, scientists can tell from a dino's bones if it was injured during its lifetime. One thing that scientists noticed about Big Al was the number of injuries that he had. Along with a few broken ribs and some injuries or infections on his feet, claws, and hips, scientists counted 19 separate injuries. So even if you're a big, bad carnivore, life at the top isn't easy. Turn to page 18 to find out why life wasn't all fun and games in the Mesozoic!

THE BARE BONES

Name: *Allosaurus*
Time period: Late Jurassic—145 million years ago
Size: 39 feet (12 m) long, 10 feet (3 m) tall, and weighed up to 2 tons.
Regions found: Western states of the U.S., like Colorado, Utah, Wyoming, and Montana.

Living on the Edge

It may seem like predators had it made at the top, but being a meat-eater wasn't easy at all! From injuries to disease to no food, there were lots of things that made life in the Mesozoic miserable for carnivores. Read on for more info!

Risky Business

Hunting wasn't a hobby for dinos—it was dangerous stuff. Plant-eating dinos weren't just waiting to be a snack! If attacked, they would defend themselves with horns, spikes, clubs, and other kinds of protection. If prey fought hard enough, they could put a hunter out for the count.

DINO DATA

In 1971, paleontologists found a fossilized fight between a *Protoceratops* (pro-toe-SER-uh-tops) and a *Velociraptor* (vee-LOSS-ih-RAP-tore). The *Velociraptor* had its claws in the *Protoceratops*'s neck, and the *Protoceratops* had bitten and broken the *Velociraptor*'s right arm. The two were duking it out when they were buried and killed by a collapsing sand dune.

Wipe Out

For you, taking a tumble might just mean some cuts and bruises. But for a big, heavy dino, a trip and fall could spell disaster. If a theropod wiped out while running after prey, it could break bones. A broken leg could prevent a dino from hunting—and surviving!

Dinos Don't Share

Theropods didn't hang out and throw parties together back in the Mesozoic. Dinos probably **competed** and fought for territory, mates, food—just about anything! This kind of fighting often ended in injury and death.

Dino Dictionary

When animals *compete*, they try to get the same thing, like food, water, or mates—things that help them (or their children) survive.

A *Ceratosaurus*
(ser-RAHT-toe-SOR-uhss)
and prey

Dino Disease

Just like other animals, dinos could get sick.
If a theropod ate prey that was infected with
disease, there was a good chance that the
hunter would catch it, too.

And there weren't any
di-nurse-aurs around,
either!

No Pit Stops

There wasn't an everlasting supply of food and
water around during the Mesozoic. Dinos had to find it—and that wasn't
easy! If a predator couldn't find food because it was hurt or because there
wasn't any, then it didn't eat. Plenty of dinos died because they starved to
death or couldn't find water.

Spinosaurus

Sails and Snouts

The next two theropods might look like crocodiles with legs, but they're all dino! Along with long snouts and lots of teeth, these two theropods had another unusual feature: a fin or "sail" along their spines.

THE BARE BONES

Name: *Spinosaurus* (SPINE-oh-SOR-uhss)

Time period: Late Cretaceous—97 million years ago

Size: *Spinosaurus* was up to 40 feet (12 m) long and weighed 3 tons. It was two-footed, and had long arms with enormous curved claws.

Regions Found: Egypt and Morocco.

A Spiny Sail

Both **Suchomimus** and **Spinosaurus** had a row of spines down their backs, which were covered by skin to make a sail. *Spinosaurus* had a huge sail—up to 6 feet (2 m) tall! But no boats for these dinos! Scientists think the sail might have been used to help *Spinosaurus* and *Suchomimus* warm up or keep cool, or it might have helped in finding a mate.

Gone Fishin'

The Mesozoic wasn't all about steak—there was seafood, too! Scientists think that *Spinosaurus* and *Suchomimus* used their long, skinny snouts to catch fish and other seafood goodies. A long snout makes it easy to snap up a slippery snack, just like modern-day crocs and alligators do. They also used their powerful arms and claws to grab whatever prey they could get their hands on!

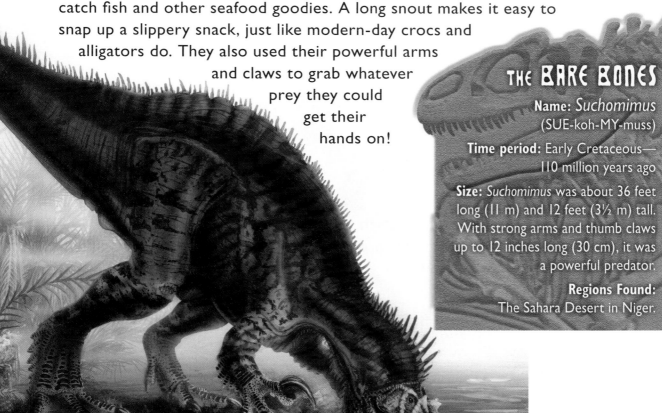

THE BARE BONES

Name: *Suchomimus* (SUE-koh-MY-muss)

Time period: Early Cretaceous—110 million years ago

Size: *Suchomimus* was about 36 feet long (11 m) and 12 feet (3½ m) tall. With strong arms and thumb claws up to 12 inches long (30 cm), it was a powerful predator.

Regions Found: The Sahara Desert in Niger.

Suchomimus

LESS IS MORE:

It's hard to believe that small theropods were in the same group as giants like *T. rex* and *Allosaurus*. But these little guys were just as fierce as their bigger buddies. Read on to discover some of their dino-mite abilities!

Zipping and Zooming

Small theropods were fierce *and* fast! Some could run up to 40 miles (64 km) per hour—that's just as fast as a racehorse! Their super-speed helped them to **catch quick-moving prey** like lizards, frogs, and other small creatures. And being light on their feet also helped them escape if they were being chased!

Thinking Theropods

Small theropods are considered to be among the **smartest dinosaurs**. Some scientists even think that they may have been smart enough to learn from their mistakes (which not every dino could do!).

Get a Grip!

Most small theropods had very **long arms** and **large hands**, which they could use to catch and hold prey, probably much better than larger theropods could.

DINO DATA

How do scientists tell if a dino was a smarty-saurus? One way to guess is to compare the size of its brain to the size of its body. If a dino had a big brain for its body size, then chances are good that it had a high dino IQ.

Dromaeosaur arms

Tyrannosaurus rex
42 ft (13 m) long

Allosaurus
39 ft (12 m) long

Deinonychus
10 ft (3 m) long

Velociraptor
6 ft (2 m) long

SMALL THEROPODS

A group of *Coelophysis*
(SEAL-oh-FIE-sis)

Killer Claw

Some small theropods had an extra-large claw on each foot called a **sickle claw**. These dinos used it to catch and kill prey. When it wasn't in use, the dinos kept it off the ground— so they were really walking on two toes instead of three.

sickle
claw
▼

Raptor foot

DINO DATA

Scientists aren't exactly sure *how* sickle claws were used. Dinos could've used sickle claws to slash their prey and kill them. Or they could've used the claw to help them jump on prey so that their arms and mouth could bite and tear. What do you think?

Dainty and Deadly

Let's meet some of the most dangerous dinos the Mesozoic has to offer. Guess what? None of them were super-sized! Why so deadly? Being big doesn't mean you're dangerous—but if you're smarter and faster than everybody else, then it's a different story! Read on to learn more!

COMPSOGNATHUS (COMP-sog-NAY-thuss)
Late Jurassic—151 million years ago

Compsognathus was about the size of a turkey, weighing only 5–7 pounds (2–3 kg). Its slim legs and long feet made *Compsognathus* a speedy little guy—it could chase

prey at up to 25 miles (40 km) an hour. Its tail was longer than its head, neck, and body put together and helped it to balance (especially during sharp turns). *Compsognathus* had tiny sharp teeth that it used to munch on the insects, snails, and lizards it caught. Yum!

Compsognathus

Dromaeosaurs (DROH-mee-oh-SORS)

These next two dinos were part of a group of theropods known as **dromaeosaurs**, which means "swift lizards." You might know them as "raptors." These vicious dinosaurs were small- to medium-sized meat-eaters with a very special feature: the ultra-wicked sickle claw.

VELOCIRAPTOR (vee-LOSS-ih-RAP-tore)
Late Cretaceous—85 million years ago

Velociraptor was 3 feet (1 m) tall and weighed about 50 pounds (23 kg). (That's about the size of a medium-sized dog.) The name *Velociraptor* means "speedy thief" and that's because—you guessed it—it was fast. This guy could sprint at 25 miles (40 km) per hour! *Velociraptor* also had a set of those cool sickle claws—one on each foot. Totally *claw*-some!

Velociraptor and Protoceratops

DEINONYCHUS (die-NON-nih-kuss)
Early Cretaceous—119 million years ago

Deinonychus was a medium-sized theropod about 5 feet (1½ m) tall and weighed in at around 175 pounds (79 kg) —about the size of a kangaroo. This powerful dinosaur was a ferocious hunter with sharp, jagged teeth, strong arms, and sharp claws. The name *Deinonychus* means "terrible claw"—meaning the sharp, curved claw on each foot. *Deinonychus* could flick its "terrible claw" in a slicing motion to catch its dinner.

DINO DATA

What's with the feathers on these dinos? Scientists think that today's birds are descended from dinos like *Deinonychus* and *Velociraptor*. Some scientists suspect that these dinos had feathers, but not the kinds that modern-day birds have. Their feathers probably kept the dinos warm and evolved for flying later.

I wouldn't want to be on the other end of that claw. Yikes!

25

A *Tenontosaurus* (teh-NON-toe-SOR-uhss) is attacked by a group of *Deinonychus*

Hunting Parties?

Some scientists think that some theropods hunted in groups. This way, they could catch much larger prey. If they bagged one of those big beasts, that meant enough food for a feast!

But not everybody thinks that pack hunting actually happened. While scientists have found herbivore dino fossils grouped together, most theropod fossils have been found solo. A lot of people think that large theropods liked being loners! And they also had another good reason not to hang out—some scientists think that some meat-eaters were **cannibals** (CAN-nih-buhls).

Dino Dictionary

Cannibals are animals that eat other animals of their own *species*, or kind.

DINO DATA

Some *Coelophysis* (see page 23 for a pic) fossils were found with the bones of other *Coelophysis* in their stomachs—that's why scientists think that *Coelophysis* were cannibals sometimes.

Take a Peek at the Beak

Oviraptor

Some small theropods had a very interesting feature that set them apart from other meat-eaters. Instead of big mouthfuls of sharp teeth, these theropods had beaks.

OVIRAPTOR (OH-vih-RAP-tore)
Late Cretaceous—85 million years ago

Oviraptor was a small theropod, about 3–4 feet (1 m) tall and weighed about 50 pounds (23 kg). Like other small theropods, *Oviraptor* could run fast—about 25 miles (40 km) per hour! Along with a parrot-shaped head and a curved crest on its nose, *Oviraptor* was totally toothless. Instead, *Oviraptor* had a pair of prongs that jutted down from the roof of its mouth. Scientists don't know what the *Oviraptor*'s diet was, but they suspect they were **omnivores** (AHM-nih-VORES).

Dino Dictionary

An *omnivore* is an animal that eats both meat and plants—they're not too picky!

What's in a Name?

In the 1920s when *Oviraptor* was discovered, many of its fossils were found near nests of dino eggs. The eggs were always empty, but scientists thought they belonged to a horned dino called *Protoceratops* and figured that *Oviraptor* was guilty of egg stealing. So scientists gave it a name that meant "egg thief." *Oviraptor* seemed like a prime suspect. It was sleek, graceful, and fast, and its beak was strong enough to crack eggs in one chomp!

Seventy years later, scientists began finding more *Oviraptor* fossils near eggs—but these eggs had *Oviraptor* babies inside! Scientists now think that this dino probably died trying to protect its own young, instead of being an egg-napper.

***Oviraptor* and babies**

DINOS IN HOLLYWOOD!

Dinos might be extinct in real life, but they're still alive and well on the movie screen! Dino movies and TV shows are as popular as ever, and while you might have figured out that dinos don't really talk (sorry Ty!), can you believe everything you see on TV? Read on for more info!

Time Traveling

Back in the day, moviemakers used to throw any two ol' dinos together for some action. For instance, an *Apatosaurus* (uh-PAT-oh-SOR-uhss) might be munching away, minding its own business when a *T. rex* charges in for the kill. Pretty exciting stuff, but guess what? This Mesozoic match-up was impossible! A *T. rex* (a Cretaceous dino) and an *Apatosaurus* (a Jurassic dino) didn't live in the same time period. They were separated by millions of years!

Nap Time

Lots of movies show meat-eating dinos tearing around, chasing prey, and making lots of noise. But instead of spending most of their time cruising for their next meal, carnivorous dinos probably did some serious snoozing! Just like the big hunters of today, dinos probably slept a lot, only hunting for a couple of hours per day. And these hunters probably didn't roar everywhere they went— it would scare off their prey!

Two dinos battle it out in the old movie *The Lost World* (1925)

A *T. rex* on the loose in *The Lost World: Jurassic Park* (1997)

Dino Dress-Up

Nowadays dinos on the screen look pretty good, thanks to computers and lots of research by animators. But before computers, moviemakers had to figure out ways to bring dinos to life on-screen. Some movies used animated puppets and others used people in rubber dino costumes. Some movies even used living lizards dressed up with plastic fins and horns to make them look strange and prehistoric.

Super-Dinos

While dinos were pretty cool to begin with (they didn't call the Mesozoic the "Age of Reptiles" for nothing!), some movies and TV shows do some improving to make them even more exciting—smarter, faster, or bigger—than they actually were.

Hey, I like the way I am! I'm DINO-mite!

ANIMATOR
YANCY F. CALZADA

Meet Yancy Calzada, an animator who's been in the business of making movies and TV shows for the last 20 years. Yancy has also worked on TV shows and movies featuring dinos, like the Disney movie *Dinosaur* (2000). Read on to learn more about how animators like Yancy put dinos on the big screen!

Q **What does a TV or movie animator do?**

A What I do is called *character animation*— I bring human and animal characters to life on-screen. This can be done with drawings, clay, or puppets. In the past, dinosaurs were usually filmed with puppets, but now we can use computers to do the same thing.

Yancy and his son Phillip in their home workshop

Q **How did you get started in dinosaur animation?**

A When I was a kid, I loved dinosaur books and movies. I'd make dinosaurs out of modeling clay and build little dino worlds with rocks and dirt. This got me interested in sculpting and painting, and then film animation, which I studied in college.

Q **What kinds of research do you do for dinosaur shows and movies?**

A The first thing I do is gather all the dinosaur books and art I can find for the newest information on how dinosaurs looked and behaved. I also study animals that have similar traits or body types of dinosaurs, like ostriches, elephants, and large reptiles. Then I try to copy the way they move when I'm animating the character.

Q **Which dinosaur project was your favorite?**

A My favorite dinosaur project was the Disney movie *Dinosaur*. I worked on that film for over three years and with a crew of over 200 people. It was really fun to go to work every day and see dinosaur art and animation by some of the most talented artists in the world.

Q **What's the hardest dinosaur project you've ever worked on?**

A Even though *Dinosaur* was the most fun, it was also the hardest. There were hundreds of dinosaurs to animate and we all spent many late nights working on it to make sure it was just right.

Two *Iguanodon* (ig-WAHN-no-don) from the Disney movie *Dinosaur* (2000)

Utahraptor

UTAHRAPTOR

In 1991, paleontologist James Kirkland got bored while waiting for his pancakes in a Utah diner and wandered into a nearby shop. He got curious about some fossils in the shop's dinosaur bone collection, so he and his team visited the site where the bones were found. With a little digging, they found a gigantic claw almost a foot (30 cm) long! Kirkland had just discovered a new dino: **Utahraptor** (YOO-tah-RAP-tore).

Utahraptor lived during the Early Cretaceous period. It was a dromaeosaur—in the same group as *Velociraptor* and *Deinonychus* (see pages 24–25). At 20 feet (6 m) long and weighing about a ton, it was possibly the deadliest of all predators. Its super-sharp sickle claw (see page 23) could measure up to 12 inches (30 cm) long! Besides being the biggest and the oldest raptor ever discovered, some scientists think that *Utahraptor* may have hunted in packs, meaning that they could catch dinos of any size.

Now that's what I call teamwork!

31

MORE DINO ADVENTURES COMING SOON!

Well, our trek with theropods has been fun! You've met meat-eaters both big and small, and become an expert in the ways of these prehistoric hunters. But there's still so much more to see! We'll dig up more fun the next time we meet for more travels through the Mesozoic. See you soon!

A young *Carcharodontosaurus* and two small theropods